EASY PIANO

40 POPULAR LOVE SONGS

ARRANGED BY DAN COATES

Project Manager: Zobeida Pérez
Cover Design: Joe Klucar

Dan Coates

As a student at the University of Miami, Dan Coates paid his tuition by playing the piano at south Florida nightclubs and restaurants. One evening in 1975, after Dan had worked his unique brand of magic on the ivories, a stranger from the music field walked up and told him that he should put his inspired piano arrangements down on paper so they could be published.

Dan took the stranger's advice—and the world of music has become much richer as a result. Since that chance encounter long ago, Dan has gone on to achieve international acclaim for his brilliant piano arrangements. His *Big Note, Easy Piano* and *Professional Touch* arrangements have inspired countless piano students and established themselves as classics against which all other works must be measured.

Enjoying an exclusive association with Warner Bros. Publications since 1982, Dan has demonstrated a unique gift for writing arrangements intended for students of every level, from beginner to advanced. Dan never fails to bring a fresh and original approach to his work. Pushing his own creative boundaries with each new manuscript, he writes material that is musically exciting and educationally sound.

From the very beginning of his musical life, Dan has always been eager to seek new challenges. As a five-year-old in Syracuse, New York, he used to sneak into the home of his neighbors to play their piano. Blessed with an amazing ear for music, Dan was able to imitate the melodies of songs he had heard on the radio. Finally, his neighbors convinced his parents to buy Dan his own piano. At that point, there was no stopping his musical development. Dan won a prestigious New York State competition for music composers at the age of 15. Then, after graduating from high school, he toured the world as an arranger and pianist with the group Up With People.

Later, Dan studied piano at the University of Miami with the legendary Ivan Davis, developing his natural abilities to stylize music on the keyboard. Continuing to perform professionally during and after his college years, Dan has played the piano on national television and at the 1984 Summer Olympics in Los Angeles. He has also accompanied recording artists as diverse as Dusty Springfield and Charlotte Rae.

During his long and prolific association with Warner Bros. Publications, Dan has written many award-winning books. He conducts piano workshops worldwide, demonstrating his famous arrangements with a special spark that never fails to inspire students and teachers alike.

BI001 2/23/04

CONTENTS

AMAZED

Words and Music by
MARV GREEN, AIMEE MAYO
and CHRIS LINDSEY
Arranged by DAN COATES

Amazed - 5 - 1

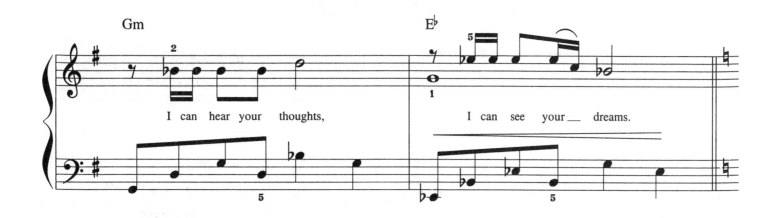

Chorus:

6

8

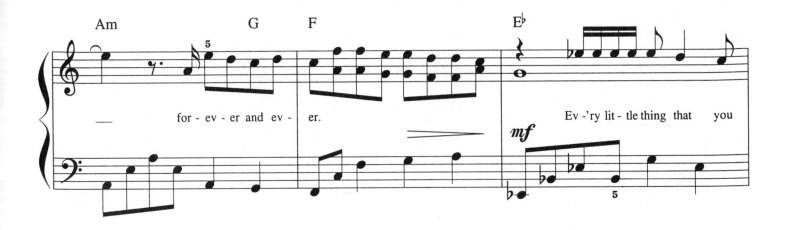

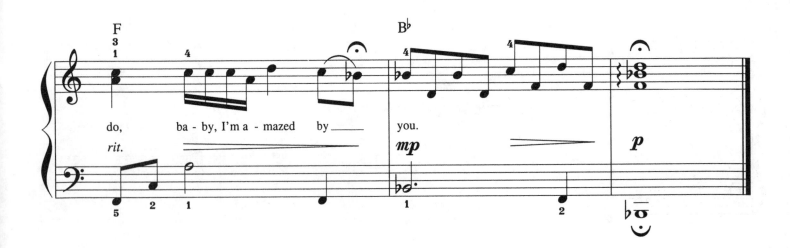

Verse 2:
The smell of your skin,
The taste of your kiss,
The way you whisper in the dark.
Your hair all around me,
Baby, you surround me.
You touch every place in my heart.
Oh, it feels like the first time every time.
I wanna spend the whole night in your eyes.
(To Chorus:)

Amazed - 5 - 5

ANGEL EYES

Composed by
JIM BRICKMAN
Arranged by DAN COATES

Angel Eyes - 3 - 1

10

ANYTHING FOR YOU

Words and Music by
GLORIA ESTEFAN
Arranged by DAN COATES

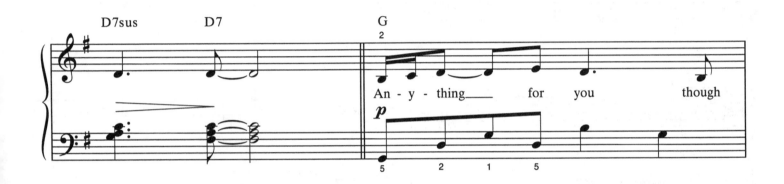

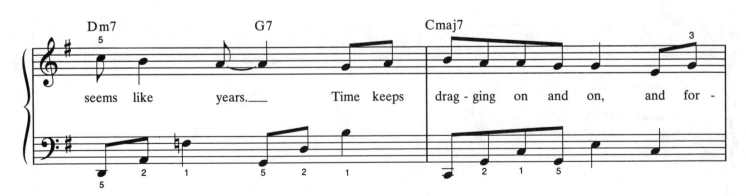

Anything for You - 5 - 1

16

BECAUSE YOU LOVED ME
(Theme from "Up Close & Personal")

Words and Music by
DIANE WARREN
Arranged by DAN COATES

Because You Loved Me - 5 - 1

18

be for-ev-er thank - ful, ba - by. You're the one ___ who held ___
grate-ful for ___ each day ___ you gave me. May - be I ___ don't know ___

___ me up, ___ nev - er let ___ me fall.
___ that much, ___ but I know this much ___ is true:

You're the one ___ who saw ___ me through,
I was blessed ___ be - cause ___ I was

through it all. ___
loved by you. ___

You were ___ my strength when I ___ was weak, you were ___ my

Because You Loved Me - 5 - 3

Because You Loved Me - 5 - 5

BEFORE YOUR LOVE

Words and Music by
DESMOND CHILD, GARY BURR
and CATHY DENNIS
Arranged by DAN COATES

Slowly (♩ = 72)

Verse:

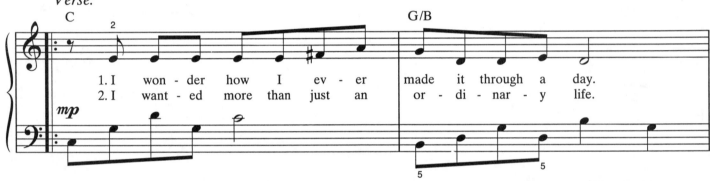

1. I won-der how I ev-er made it through a day.
2. I want-ed more than just an or-di-nar-y life.

How did I set-tle for a world in shades of gray?
All of my dreams seemed like cas-tles in the sky.

When you go in cir-cles, all the scen-'ry looks the same and you don't know
I stand be-fore you and my heart is in your hands and I don't know

Before Your Love - 4 - 1

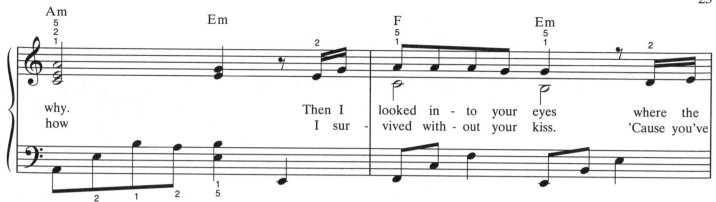

why. | Then I | looked in-to your eyes | where the
how | I sur - vived with-out your kiss. | 'Cause you've

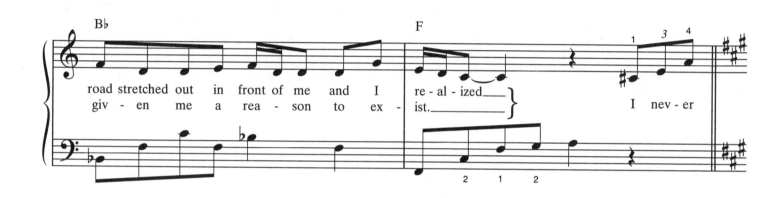

road stretched out in front of me and I | re - al - ized___ | I nev - er
giv - en me a rea - son to ex - | ist.___ |

%⁣ *Chorus:*

lived___ | be - fore your | love. | I nev - er

mf

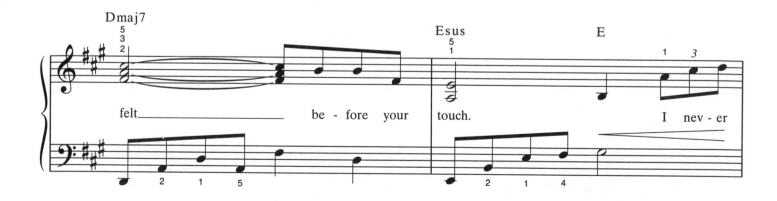

felt___ | be - fore your | touch. | I nev - er

Before Your Love - 4 - 2

24

C
G/B
mf
And I don't know
Am
Em
F
Em
why, why the sun de - cides to shine, but you
B♭
Fmaj7
D.S. al Coda
breathed your love in - to me just in time. I nev - er
Coda
Bm7
E7
lived, I nev - er lived be - fore your
mf
A
D/A
A
love.
mp
rit. e dim.
p

DON'T KNOW MUCH
(aka All I Need to Know)

Lyric by
CYNTHIA WEIL

Music by
TOM SNOW and BARRY MANN
Arranged by DAN COATES

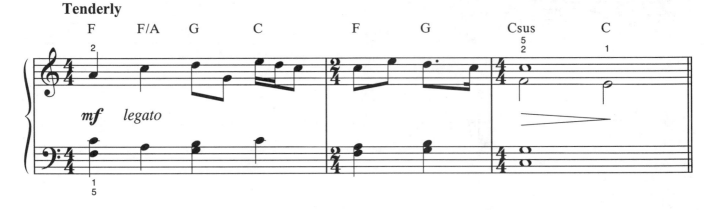

Look at this face,
Look at these eyes,

I know the years are show - ing.
they've nev - er seen what mat - ters.

Look at this life,___
Look at these dreams,___

I still don't know where it's go - ing.
so beat - en and so bat - tered.

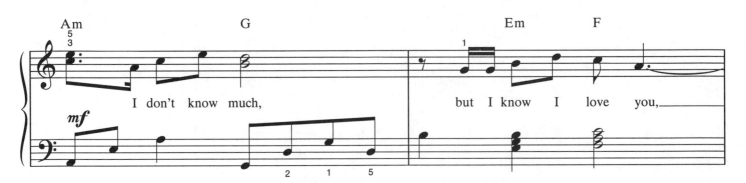

I don't know much,

but I know I love you,___

Don't Know Much - 4 - 1

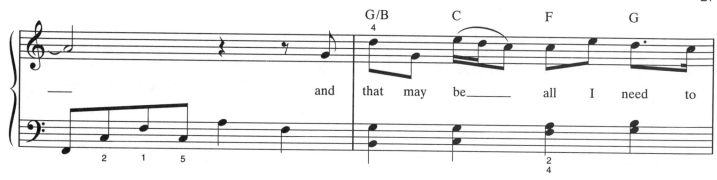

and that may be_____ all I need to

1.
know.

2.
know.

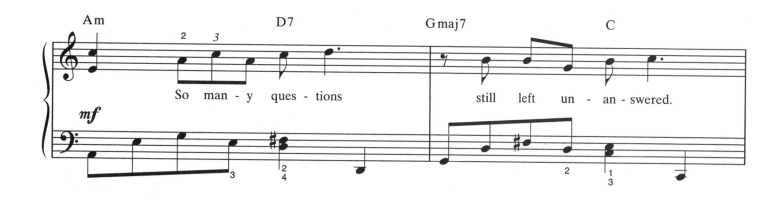

So man-y ques-tions still left un-an-swered.

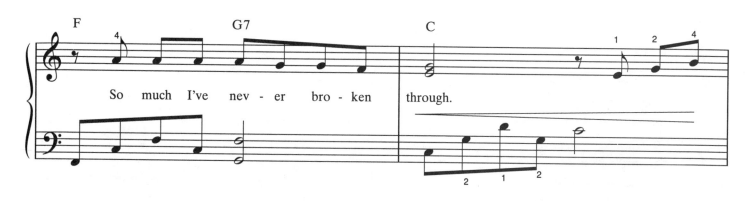

So much I've nev-er bro-ken through.

DREAMING OF YOU

Words and Music by
TOM SNOW and FRANNE GOLDE
Arranged by DAN COATES

32

8TH WORLD WONDER

Words and Music by
KYLE JACOBS, SHAUN SHANKEL
and JOEL PARKES
Arranged by DAN COATES

With a moderate, steady beat (♩ = 100)

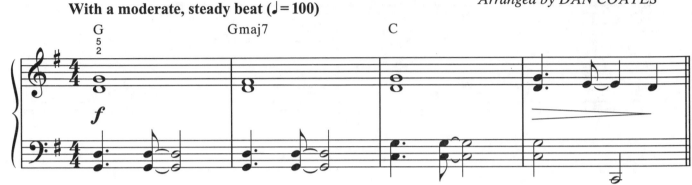

Verse:

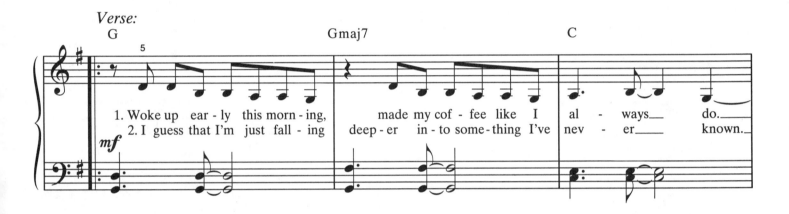

1. Woke up ear-ly this morn-ing, made my cof-fee like I al-ways___ do.___
2. I guess that I'm just fall-ing deep-er in-to some-thing I've nev-er___ known.___

Then it hit me from no-where, ev-'ry-thing I feel a-bout
But the way that I'm feel-ing makes me re-al-ize that it

me and___ you.___ The way___ you
can't be___ wrong.___ Your love's like a

8th World Wonder - 4 - 1

Chorus:

36

Yeah, yeah, yeah. It's on-ly been a week but, it's com-ing o-ver me, yeah.

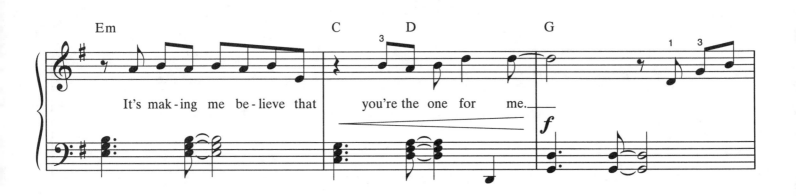

It's mak-ing me be-lieve that you're the one for me.

8th World Wonder - 4 - 3

FOR YOU I WILL

Words and Music by
DIANE WARREN
Arranged by DAN COATES

40

D.S. 𝄋 al Coda

give my word, I'll give it all. Put your faith in me, I'll do an - y - thing. I will cross the

Coda

will. Prom - ise you, for you I

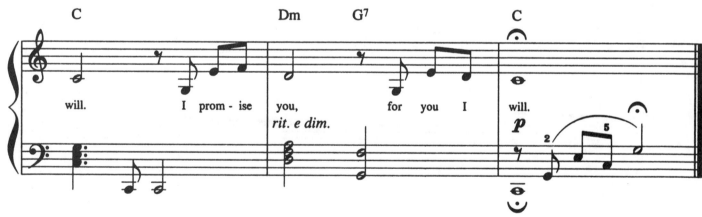

will. I prom - ise you, for you I will.

rit. e dim.

Verse 2:
I will shield your heart from the rain,
I won't let no harm come your way.
Oh, these arms will be your shelter,
No, these arms won't let you down.
If there is a mountain to move,
I will move that mountain for you.
I'm here for you, I'm here forever.
I will be a fortress, tall and strong.
I'll keep you safe, I'll stand beside you,
Right or wrong.   *(To Chorus:)*

(I Wanna Take)
FOREVER TONIGHT

Words and Music by
ANDY GOLDMARK and ERIC CARMEN
Arranged by DAN COATES

Verse:

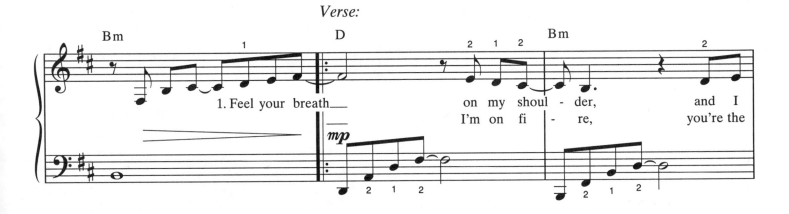

1. Feel your breath___ on my shoul - der, and I

I'm on fi - re, you're the

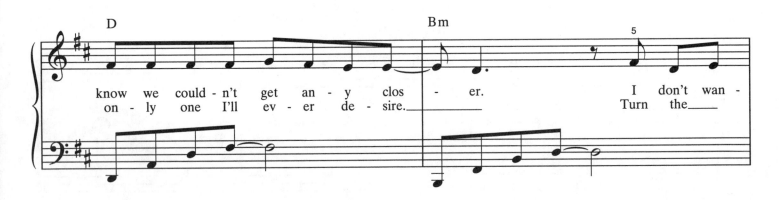

know we could-n't get an-y clos - er. I don't wan -

on - ly one I'll ev-er de - sire.___ Turn the___

na act tough,___ I just wan - na fall in love.___ As we move___

light down low, make the___ world go___ slow. When I'm hold -

46

I GET WEAK

Words and Music by
DIANE WARREN
Arranged by DAN COATES

Moderate rock ballad

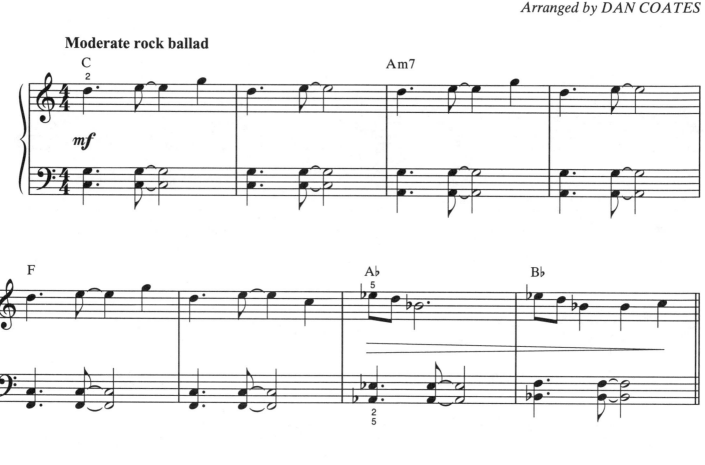

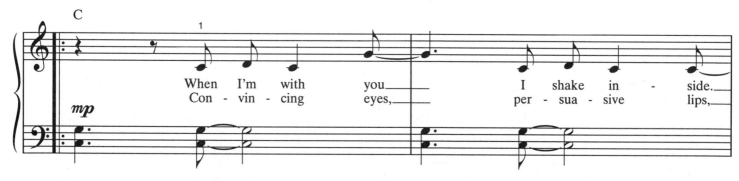

When I'm with you____ I shake in - side.____
Con - vin - cing eyes,____ per - sua - sive lips,____

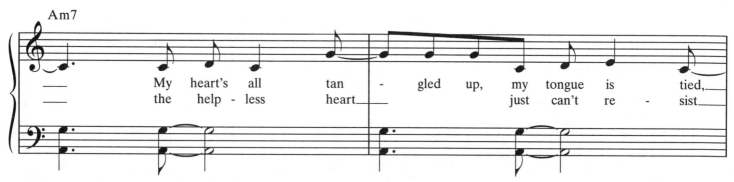

My heart's all tan - gled up, my tongue is tied,
the help - less heart just can't re - sist

I Get Weak - 5 - 1

48

I Get Weak - 5 - 2

51

I Get Weak - 5 - 5

HOLD ON TO THE NIGHTS

Words and Music by
RICHARD MARX
Arranged by DAN COATES

HOW DO I LIVE

Words and Music by
DIANE WARREN
Arranged by DAN COATES

How Do I Live - 4 - 1

Verse 2:
Without you, there'd be no sun in my sky,
There would be no love in my life,
There'd be no world left for me.
And I, baby, I don't know what I would do,
I'd be lost if I lost you.
If you ever leave,
Baby, you would take away everything
Real in my life.
And tell me now...
(To Chorus:)

How Do I Live - 4 - 4

I DON'T WANT TO MISS A THING

Words and Music by
DIANE WARREN
Arranged by DAN COATES

I HAVE NOTHING

Words and Music by
LINDA THOMPSON and DAVID FOSTER
Arranged by DAN COATES

I Have Nothing - 5 - 1

68

Have Nothing - 5 - 5

LOOK AWAY

Words and Music by
DIANE WARREN
Arranged by DAN COATES

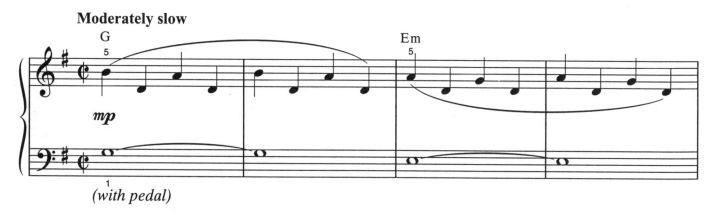

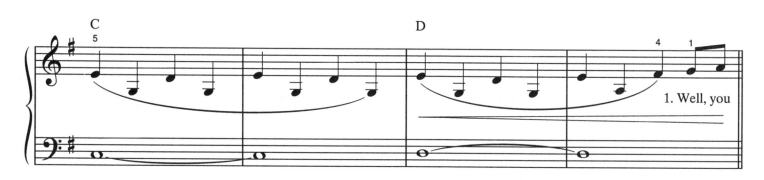

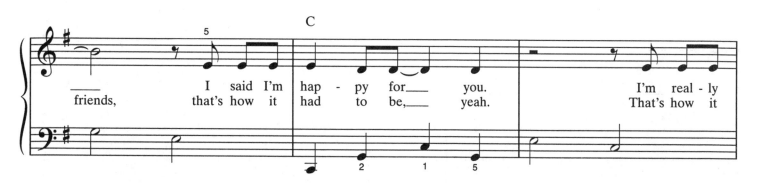

Look Away - 5 - 1

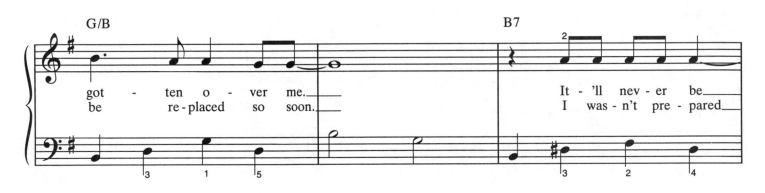

72

Look Away - 5 - 4

I'M ALIVE

Words and Music by
KRISTIAN LUNDIN and ANDREAS CARLSSON
Arranged by DAN COATES

With a moderate, steady beat (♩ = 104)

Mmm. Mmm.

I get wings to fly,

oh,_____ I'm a-live. When you

%. *Chorus:*

call on me,_____ when I hear you breathe,_____

I'm Alive - 5 - 1

I WILL ALWAYS LOVE YOU

Words and Music by
DOLLY PARTON
Arranged by DAN COATES

I Will Always Love You - 3 - 1

80

Extra Lyrics:

3. I hope life treats you kind
   And I hope you have all you've dreamed of.
   I wish you joy and happiness.
   But above all this,
   I wish you love.

LOVE IS

Words and Music by
JOHN KELLER, TONIO K.
and MICHAEL CARUSO
Arranged by DAN COATES

They say it's a riv-er that cir-cles the earth,

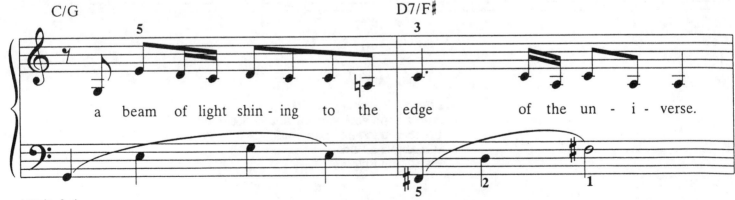

a beam of light shin-ing to the edge of the un-i-verse.

Love Is - 6 - 1

It con - quers all.____ It chang - es ev -

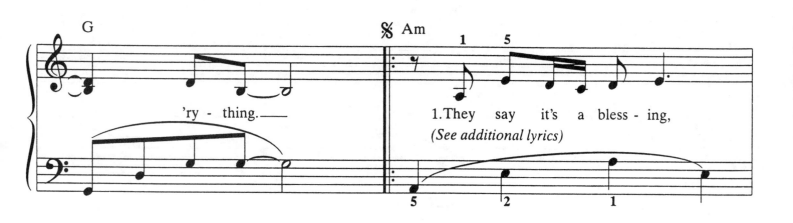

'ry - thing.____

1. They say it's a bless - ing,
(See additional lyrics)

they say it's a gift. They say it's a mir - a - cle, and I be -

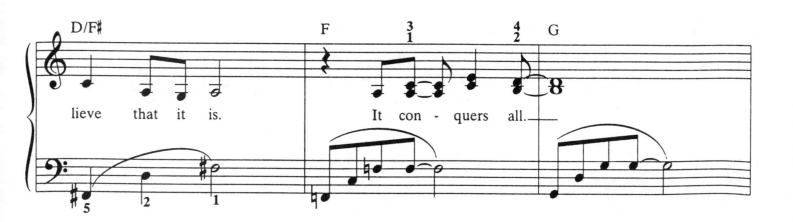

lieve that it is. It con - quers all.____

Love Is - 6 - 2

86

Love Is - 6 - 5

Additional Lyrics:

2. In this world we've created,
   In this place that we live,
   In the blink of an eye, babe,
   The darkness slips in.
   Love lights the world,
   Unites the lovers for eternity.

   Love breaks the chains.
   Love aches for every one of us.
   Love takes the tears and the pain
   And it turns it into
   The beauty that remains.

Love Is - 6 - 6

LOVE WILL KEEP US ALIVE

Words and Music by
JIM CAPALDI, PETER VALE
and PAUL CARRACK
Arranged by DAN COATES

Moderately slow ♩ = 88

Love Will Keep Us Alive - 4 - 1

90

Love Will Keep Us Alive - 4 - 3

Love Will Keep Us Alive - 4 - 4

LOVE WILL LEAD YOU BACK

Words and Music by
DIANE WARREN
Arranged by DAN COATES

Slowly, with expression

Say - ing good-

bye_____ is nev - er an eas - y thing,__ but you ne - ver
nights_____ I'll hear your voice a - gain,__ you're gon - na

said_____ that you'd stay for - ev - er.__ So, if you must
say_____ how much you missed me.__ You'll walk out this

Love Will Lead You Back - 5 - 1

94

2.
C
G/C
B♭
back.
mf
mp
E♭/B♭
B♭
E♭/B♭
B♭
F/A
cresc.
Gm7
F/G
Cm7
B♭/D
I won't try to stop you now from leav-ing, 'cause
E♭
Dm/G
G
D.S. al Coda
in my heart I know,
Love will lead you

MEET ME HALFWAY

Words by
TOM WHITLOCK

Music by
GIORGIO MORODER
Arranged by DAN COATES

Meet Me Halfway - 3 - 1

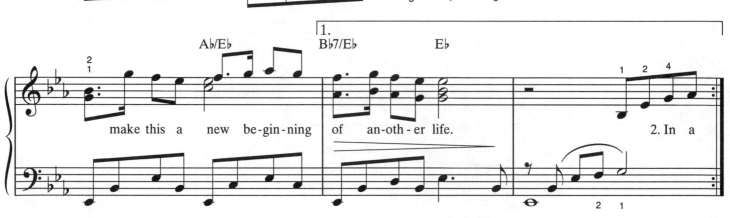

got the fu - ture on my mind,
put e - mo - tions on the line,

know that you'll be the on - ly one.
know that we are the time - less ones.

cresc.

Meet me half way

a - cross the sky,

out where the world be - longs to on - ly you and I.

Meet me half way

a - cross the sky,

make this a new be - gin - ning of an - oth - er life.

2. In a

MENTAL PICTURE

Words and Music by
JON SECADA and
MIGUEL A. MOREJON
Arranged by DAN COATES

Mental Picture - 3 - 1

Verse 2:
Time was of the essence,
And as usual the day turns into minutes.
Sharing love and tenderness,
That's the nerve you struck in me that sent a signal.
To the other side,
(Girl, I don't know)
Saying my blind side.
And if a ... *(To Chorus:)*

NOW AND FOREVER

Words and Music by
RICHARD MARX
Arranged by DAN COATES

Now and Forever - 3 - 1

MISSING YOU NOW

Words and Music by
MICHAEL BOLTON, WALTER AFANASIEFF
and DIANE WARREN
Arranged by DAN COATES

Missing You Now - 4 - 1

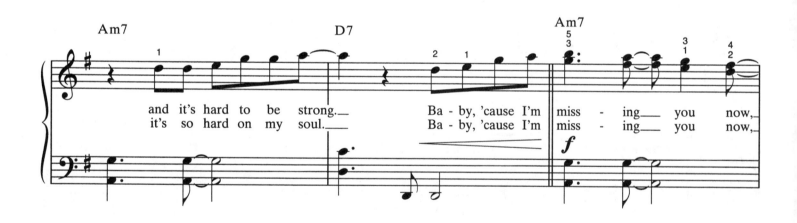

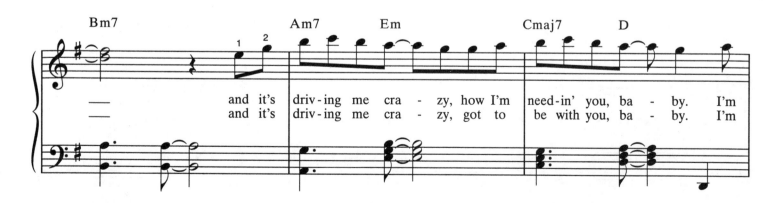

Missing You Now - 4 - 2

NOTHING'S GONNA STOP US NOW

Words and Music by
ALBERT HAMMOND and DIANE WARREN
Arranged by DAN COATES

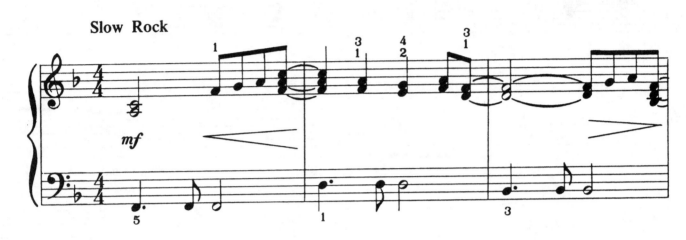

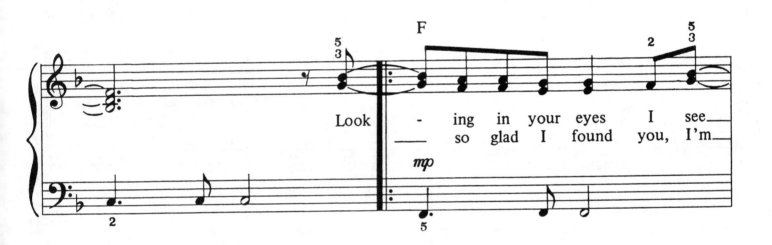

Look - ing in your eyes I see
___ so glad I found you, I'm___

___ a par - a - dise, this world ___ that I found ___ is too good ___
___ not gon - na lose you. What - ev - er it takes ___ I will stay ___

Nothing's Gonna Stop Us Now - 6 - 1

112

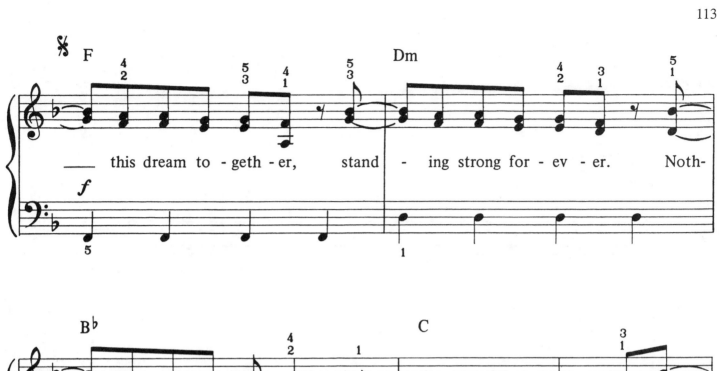

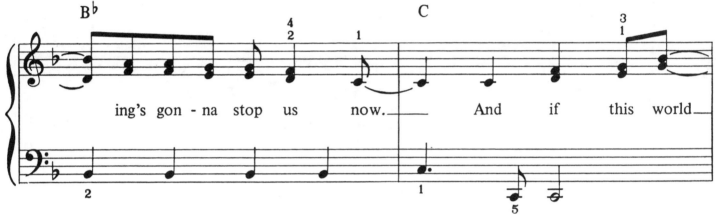

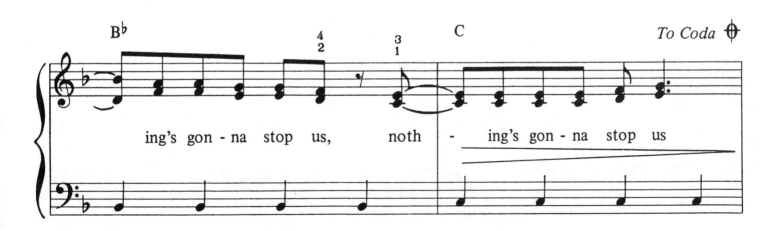

114

115

SET THE NIGHT TO MUSIC

Words and Music by
DIANE WARREN
Arranged by DAN COATES

Set the Night to Music - 5 - 1

120

Additional Lyrics

Let's find a rhythm all our own,
Melt into it nice and slow.
Love ourselves away from here.
Your heart beating next to mine,
Perfect love in perfect time.
Watch the world just disappear.
The moment is ours to take,
And with the love we make
We could.... (to Chorus)

Set the Night to Music - 5 - 5

From Touchstone Pictures' "PEARL HARBOR"

THERE YOU'LL BE

Words and Music by
DIANE WARREN
Arranged by DAN COATES

Slowly (♩ = 69)

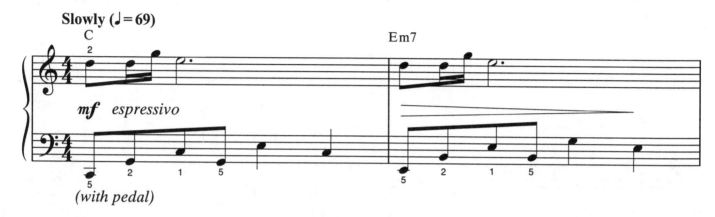

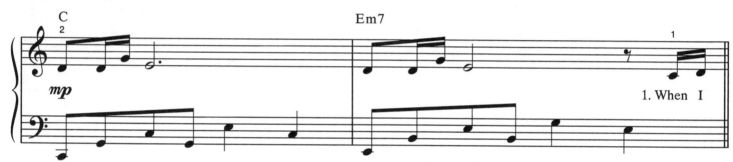

Verse:

There You'll Be - 5 - 1

122

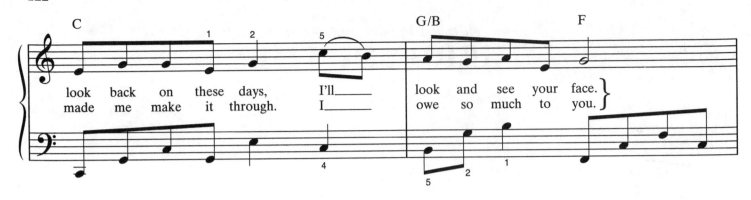

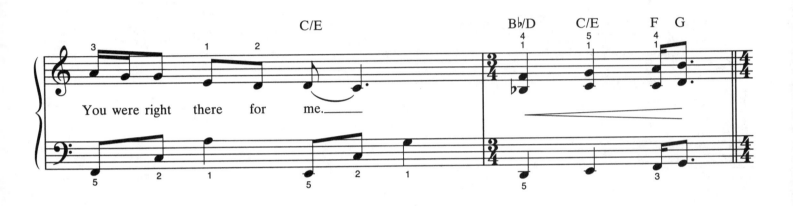

Chorus:

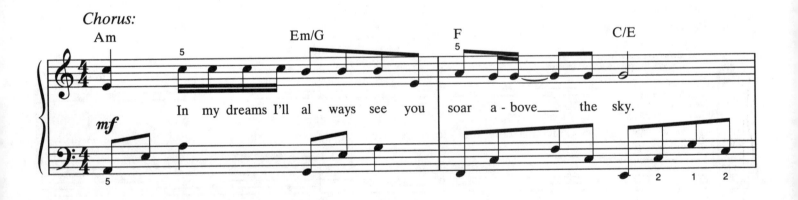

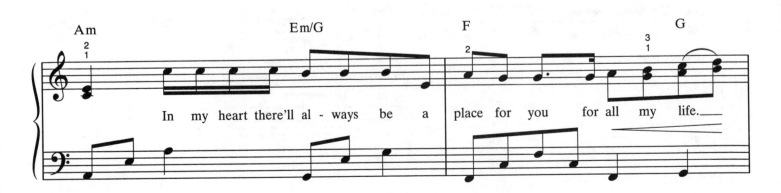

There You'll Be - 5 - 2

123

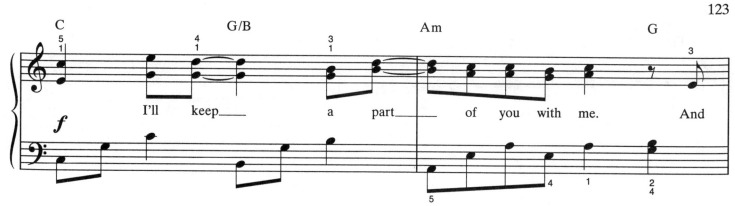

I'll keep____ a part____ of you with me. And

1.
ev-'ry-where I am, there you'll be.____ And

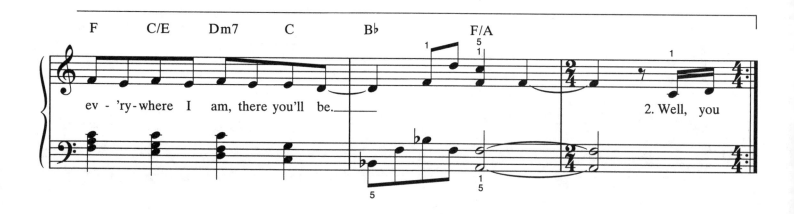

ev-'ry-where I am, there you'll be.____ 2. Well, you

2.
ev-'ry-where I am, there you'll be.____ 'Cause I al-ways saw in you my

There You'll Be - 5 - 3

124

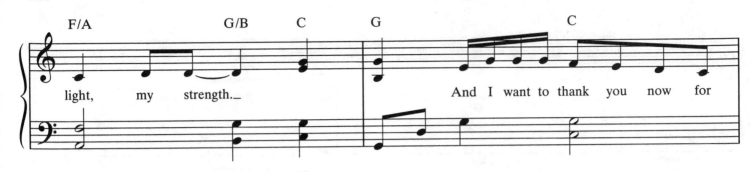

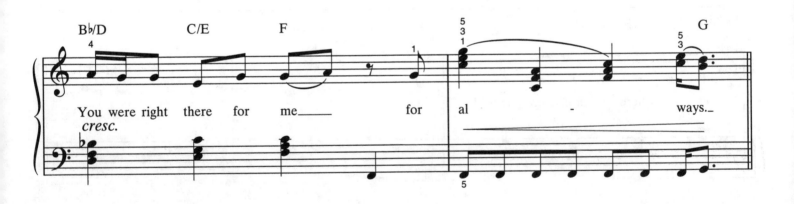

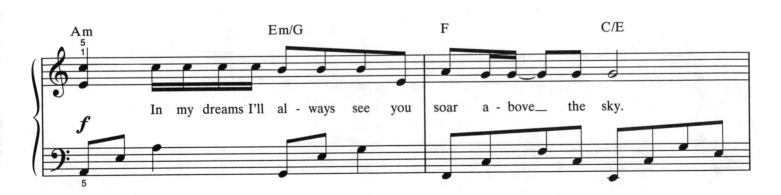

There You'll Be - 5 - 4

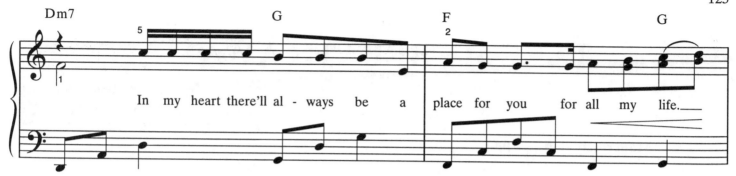

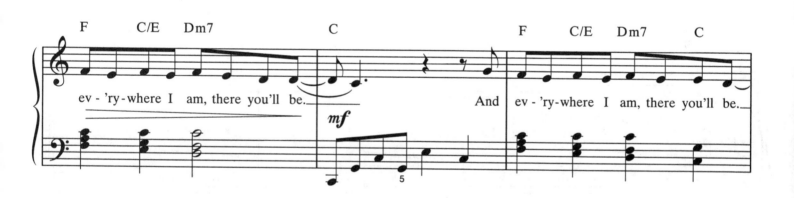

There You'll Be - 5 - 5

TAKE MY BREATH AWAY

By
GIORGIO MORODER and TOM WHITLOCK
Arranged by DAN COATES

Moderately slow (♩ = 100)

Verse:

1. Watch-ing ev - 'ry mo - tion in
2. Watch-ing, I keep wait - ing, still

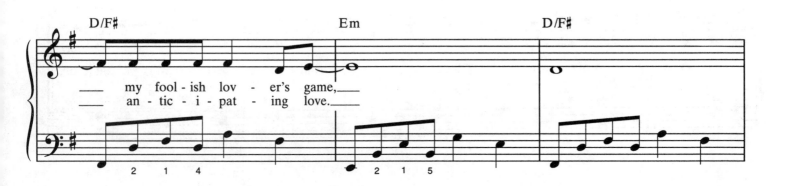

___ my fool - ish lov - er's game,___
___ an - tic - i - pat - ing love.___

on this end - less o - cean, fi - n'lly lov - ers know no shame.___
Nev - er hes - i - tat - ing to___ be - come the fat - ed one.___

Take My Breath Away - 4 - 1

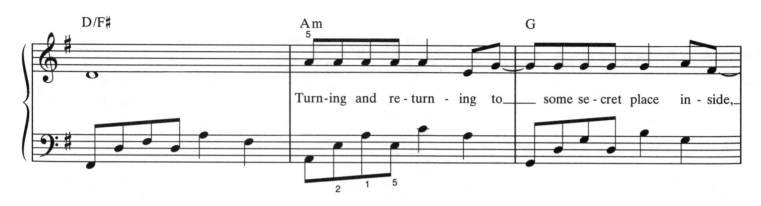

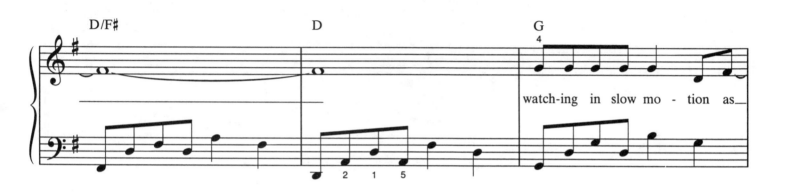

Chorus:

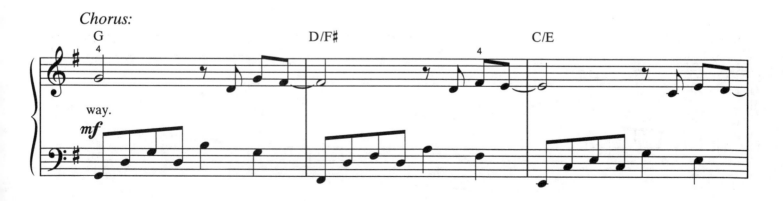

Take My Breath Away - 4 - 2

128

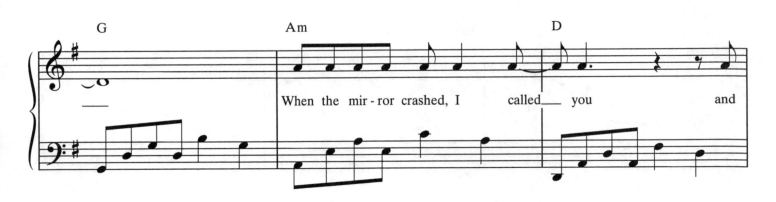

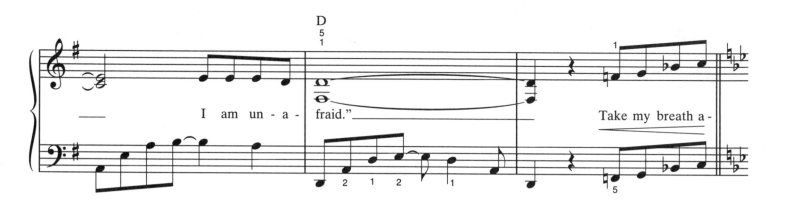

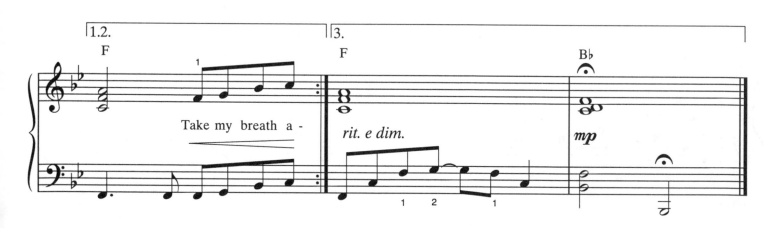

Take My Breath Away - 4 - 4

THIS I PROMISE YOU

Words and Music by
RICHARD MARX
Arranged by DAN COATES

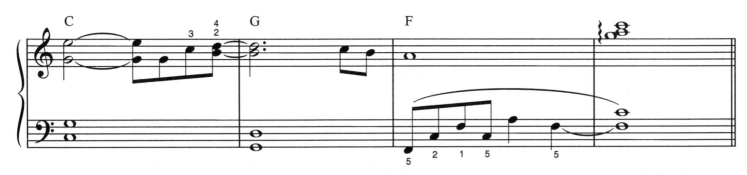

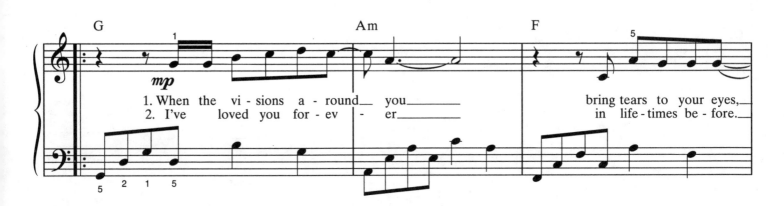

1. When the vi-sions a-round you bring tears to your eyes,
2. I've loved you for-ev - er in life-times be-fore.

and all that sur-rounds you
And I prom-ise you, nev - er

This I Promise You - 4 - 1

THIS IS THE NIGHT

Words and Music by
CHRISTOPHER BRAIDE, GARY BURR
and ALDO NOVA
Arranged by DAN COATES

Majestically (♩= 50)

1. When the world was-n't up - side down, I could

take all the time I had. But I'm not gon-na wait when a mo-

ment can van - ish so fast. 'Cause

This Is the Night - 5 - 1

This Is the Night - 5 - 2

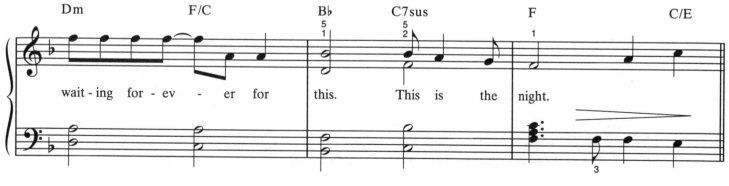

138

TO WHERE YOU ARE

Words and Music by
RICHARD MARX and
LINDA THOMPSON
Arranged by DAN COATES

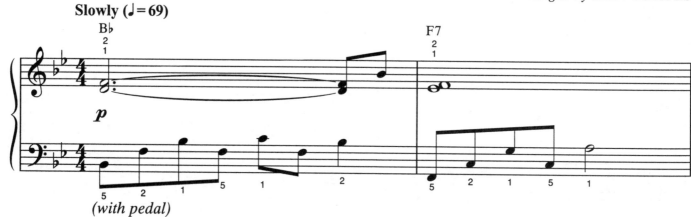

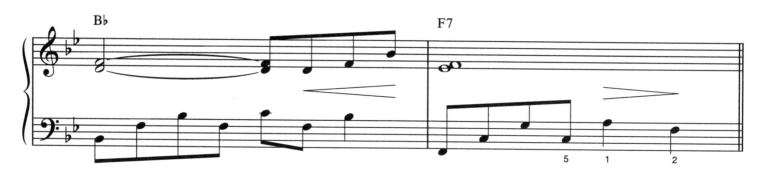

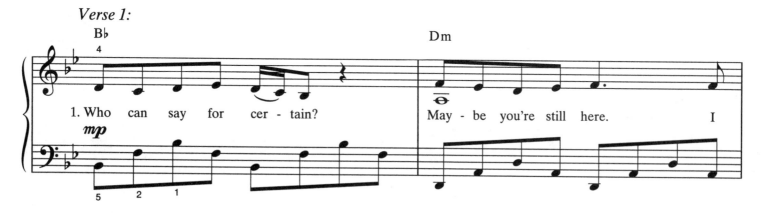

To Where You Are - 5 - 1

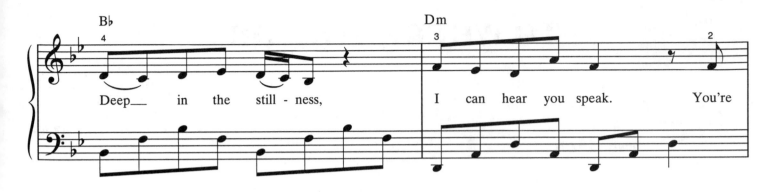

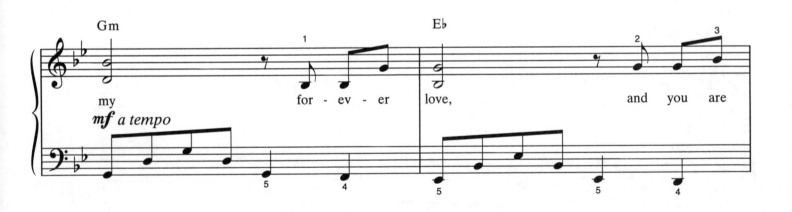

To Where You Are - 5 - 3

To Where You Are - 5 - 5

VALENTINE

Composed by
JIM BRICKMAN
and JACK KUGELL
Arranged by DAN COATES

Valentine - 4 - 1

146

Verse 2:
All of my life,
I have been waiting for all you give to me.
You've opened my eyes
And shown me how to love unselfishly.
I've dreamed of this a thousand times before,
But in my dreams I couldn't love you more.
I will give you my heart until the end of time.
You're all I need, my love,
My Valentine.

UN-BREAK MY HEART

Words and Music by
DIANE WARREN
Arranged by DAN COATES

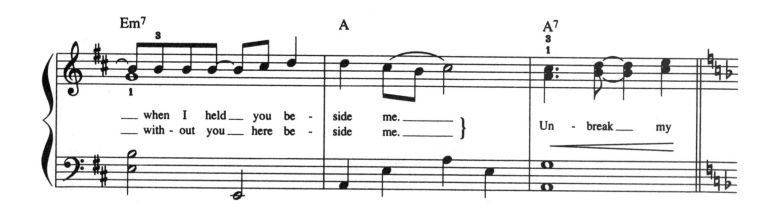

150

152

Come back ___ and say you love me. Un - break ___ my

heart, sweet dar - ling. With - out you, I just can't go on. ___

THE WAY

Words and Music by
**DAVID SIEGEL, STEVE MORALES,
KARA DIOGUARDI** and **ENRIQUE IGLESIAS**
Arranged by DAN COATES

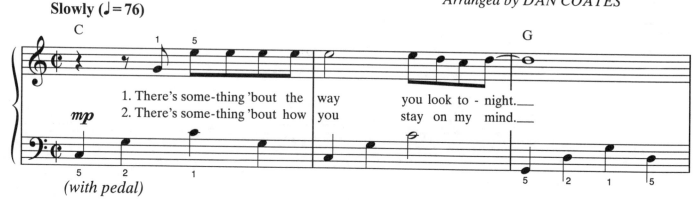

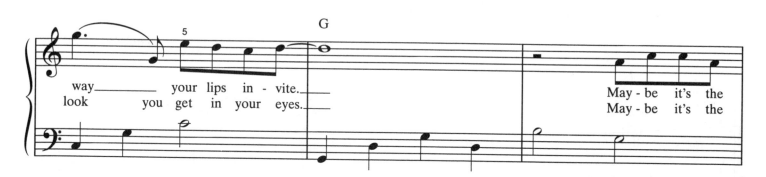

The Way - 5 - 1

makes me love you. So don't ask me to de - scribe. I get all choked up in - side just think - ing 'bout the way. It's in the way that you move me and the way that you tease me, the way that I want you to - night.

WHEN A MAN LOVES A WOMAN

Words and Music by
ANDREW WRIGHT and CALVIN LEWIS
Arranged by DAN COATES

When a man ___ loves a wom - an, ___ can't keep his mind on noth- in' else. He'd trade the world for the good thing he's

man ___ loves a wom - an, ___ spend his ver - y last dime try - ing to hold on to what he

When a Man Loves a Woman - 4 - 1

160

Coda

Play 3 times

When a man loves a woman.

Additional Lyrics
When a man loves a woman,
Deep down in his soul,
She can bring him such misery.
If she is playing him for a fool,
He's the last one to know.
Loving eyes can never see.

When a Man Loves a Woman - 4 - 4

WHEN YOU LIE NEXT TO ME

Words and Music by
KELLIE COFFEY, TRINA HARMON
and J.D. MARTIN
Arranged by DAN COATES

When You Lie Next to Me - 3 - 1

163

When You Lie Next to Me - 3 - 2

164

When You Lie Next to Me - 3 - 3

YOU NEEDED ME

Words and Music by
RANDY GOODRUM
Arranged by DAN COATES

Slowly, with expression

1. I cried a tear, you wiped it dry.
I was con-
fused, you cleared my mind.
I sold my soul
you bought it
back for me, and held me up
and gave me
dig - ni - ty. Some-how you

hand when it was cold.
When I was
lost, you took me home.
You gave me hope
when I was
at the end, and turned my lies
back in - to truth a - gain.
You e - ven

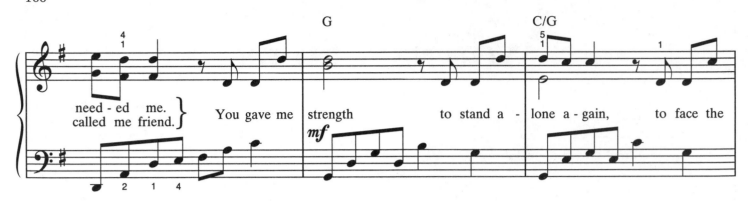

need - ed me. / called me friend. You gave me strength to stand a - lone a - gain, to face the

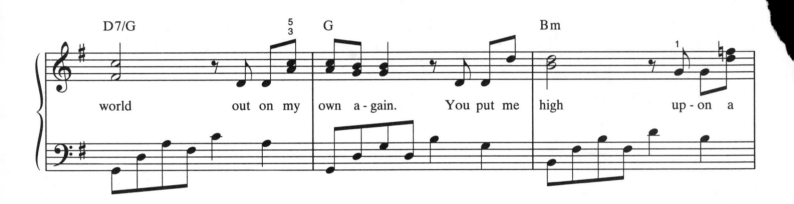

world out on my own a - gain. You put me high up - on a

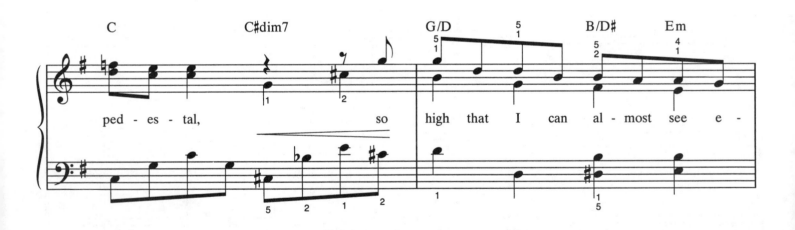

ped - es - tal, so high that I can al - most see e -

To Coda ⊕

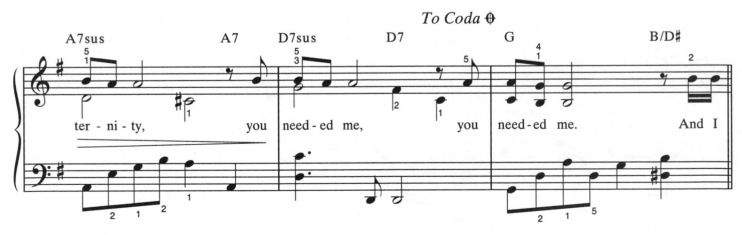

ter - ni - ty, you need - ed me, you need - ed me. And I

YOU RAISE ME UP

Words and Music by
ROLF LOVLAND and BRENDAN GRAHAM
Arranged by DAN COATES

You Raise Me Up - 4 - 1

169

You Raise Me Up - 4 - 2

Chorus:

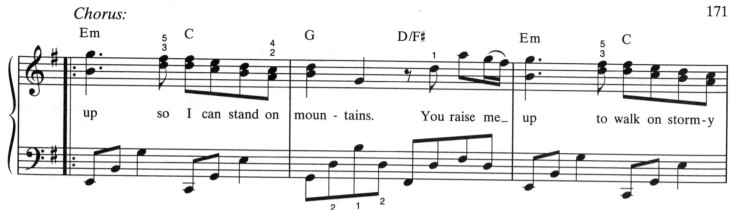

up   so I can stand on moun - tains.   You raise me_ up   to walk on storm-y

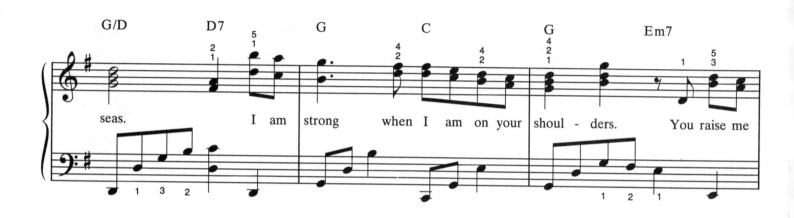

seas.   I am strong   when I am on your shoul - ders.   You raise me

up   to more than I can   be.   You raise me   be._

— You raise me up   to more than_ I can   be.

ANOTHER SAD LOVE SONG

By
DARYL SIMMONS and BABYFACE
Arranged by DAN COATES

Since you been gone, I been hang-in' a-round— here late-
Since you been gone, I keep think-in' a-bout— you, ba-

174

176

Another Sad Love Song - 5 - 5